Peace in the Valley

Weekly Devotionals for Those Who Grieve

ALI PASKUN

Published by Amazon KDP

Cover Design: Robin K. Axtell
Photos: Emily Jordan and Marty Williams
Editing/Interior Design: Michele Chynoweth

ISBN: 9798218560041

Dedication

I dedicate this book to those who have had to experience a
journey through grief. While I don't know the details of your
specific circumstance, I do know grief is often so
overwhelming that you can feel lost, confused, and
sorrowful. I also know there is no greater Comforter than
our Lord. I pray the contents of this book will help you find
solace so you can rest in His arms
and find peace.
I also dedicate it to my husband Bill who went home to the
Lord in 2014. I treasure the memories of our years together. I
will love and miss you until we are reunited, never to be
apart again.

Ali Paskun

Acknowledgements

Most important, praise to my Lord and Savior Jesus Christ
who has supported and encouraged me through my life thus
far and will continue to do so until He calls me home.
To Him be the glory! Thanks to my 420 Fire Maryland family
who encouraged me to pursue my vision for this book.
I appreciate the talents of Robin K. Axtell for the cover
design, Emily Jordan for the author photograph and
Marty Williams for graphics support. This book would
have never made it over the goal line without my
Book Coach Michele Chynoweth's editing and
publishing assistance.
To my brother, Tony Malanowski—you're the best and
I'm blessed to have you in my corner always. Finally, my
eternal gratitude to the family and friends who have been
there for me when I've grieved.

Week One Reflection:

Journal your thoughts throughout the week as you reflect on the devotional or scripture passage on the following page:

_____

_____

_____

_____

_____

_____

_____

_____

_____

_____

_____

_____

Trust in God

"When the grief is fresh and intense, we might take some wild ideas for a test drive, but to move forward toward healing and return to joy requires that we press this one idea deeply into our souls until it begins to impact us at the level of our feelings:
'I can trust God with this'."
Nancy Guthrie[1]

Week Two Reflection:

Journal your thoughts throughout the week as you reflect on the
devotional or scripture passage on the following page:

_____

_____

_____

_____

_____

_____

_____

_____

_____

_____

_____

Cast Your Burden

"Cast your burden on the Lord, And He
shall sustain you;
He shall never permit the righteous
to be moved."
Psalm 55:22

Week Three Reflection:

Journal your thoughts throughout the week as you reflect on the devotional or scripture passage on the following page:

_____

_____

_____

_____

_____

_____

_____

_____

_____

_____

_____

_____

Believe in Glory

"For I consider that the sufferings
of this present time are not
worthy to be compared with the
glory which shall be revealed in us."
Romans 8:18

Week Four Reflection:

Journal your thoughts throughout the week as you reflect on the devotional or scripture passage on the following page:

_____

_____

_____

_____

_____

_____

_____

_____

_____

_____

_____

You Will Be Comforted

"Blessed are those who mourn, for they
shall be comforted."
Matthew 5:4

Week Five Reflection:

Journal your thoughts throughout the week as you reflect on the
devotional or scripture passage on the following page:

_____

_____

_____

_____

_____

_____

_____

_____

_____

_____

_____

The Lord Is Near

"The Lord is near to those who have
a broken heart, and saves such as are
crushed in spirit."
Psalm 34:18

Week Six Reflection:

Journal your thoughts throughout the week as you reflect on the
devotional or scripture passage on the following page:

_____

_____

_____

_____

_____

_____

_____

_____

_____

_____

Comfort Others As Well

"Blessed be the God and Father of our Lord Jesus Christ, the Father of mercies and God of all comfort, who comforts us in all our tribulation, that we may be able to comfort those who are in any trouble, with the comfort with which we ourselves are comforted by God."
2 Corinthians 1:3-4

Week Seven Reflection:

Journal your thoughts throughout the week as you reflect on the
devotional or scripture passage on the following page:

_____

_____

_____

_____

_____

_____

_____

_____

_____

_____

_____

_____

Jesus Understands

"Scripture tells us Jesus '…made Himself of no reputation, taking the form of a bondservant, and coming in the likeness of men.' (Philippians 2:7). He understands. He felt grief and wept on learning His friend Lazarus had died, even knowing that He would raise Lazarus. He understands your feelings and emotions. He hears you cry. He is ready to hold you and bear your grief with you. Take it all to Him. He is ready to bear what you find unbearable."

Ali Paskun

Week Eight Reflection:

Journal your thoughts throughout the week as you reflect on the
devotional or scripture passage on the following page:

_____

_____

_____

_____

_____

_____

_____

_____

_____

_____

_____

He Will Save

"Surely He has borne our griefs and
carried our sorrows;
Yet we esteemed Him stricken, Smitten
by God, and afflicted."
Isaiah 53:4

Week Nine Reflection:

Journal your thoughts throughout the week as you reflect on the
devotional or scripture passage on the following page:

_____

_____

_____

_____

_____

_____

_____

_____

_____

_____

_____

He Will Give You Rest

"Come to me, all who labor and are heavy
laden, and I will give you rest. Take my
yoke upon you, and learn from me, for I
am gentle and lowly in heart, and you will
find rest for your souls. For my yoke is
easy, and my burden is light."
Matthew 11:28-30

Week Ten Reflection:

Journal your thoughts throughout the week as you reflect on the
devotional or scripture passage on the following page:

_____

_____

_____

_____

_____

_____

_____

_____

_____

_____

_____

_____

Have Mercy, Lord

"Have mercy on me, O Lord, for I am in trouble;
My eye wastes away with grief, Yes, my soul and
my body! For my life is spent with grief, And my
years with sighing; My strength fails
because of my iniquity, and
my bones waste away."
Psalm 31:9-10

Week Eleven Reflection:

Journal your thoughts throughout the week as you reflect on the
devotional or scripture passage on the following page:

_____

_____

_____

_____

_____

_____

_____

_____

_____

_____

_____

_____

Your Strength

"My flesh and my heart fail;
But God is the strength of my heart
and my portion forever."
Psalm 73:26

Week Twelve Reflection:

Journal your thoughts throughout the week as you reflect on the
devotional or scripture passage on the following page:

_____

_____

_____

_____

_____

_____

_____

_____

_____

_____

_____

Be Not Afraid

"Have I not commanded you?
Be strong and of good courage;
do not be afraid, nor be dismayed,
for the Lord your God
is with you wherever you go."

Joshua 1:9

Week Thirteen Reflection:

Journal your thoughts throughout the week as you reflect on the devotional or scripture passage on the following page:

_____

_____

_____

_____

_____

_____

_____

_____

_____

_____

_____

_____

Prayer of Grief

"Father, I come to you now to cast my grief, my
sorrow, my loneliness,
and my pain before Your throne.
I feel so lost now as I face another
day without my loved one.
While I rejoice in the memories I have,
I mourn the memories that will never be.
I need You, Lord. Grant me
the strength, courage, and peace
I need to move forward with my life.
In Jesus name. Amen."

Ali Paskun

Week Fourteen Reflection:

Journal your thoughts throughout the week as you reflect on the devotional or scripture passage on the following page:

_____

_____

_____

_____

_____

_____

_____

_____

_____

_____

_____

_____

The Resurrection and the Life

"Jesus said to her, 'I am the resurrection and the life.
He who believes in Me, though he may die, he shall
live. And whoever lives and believes in Me
shall never die. Do you believe this?'"

John 11:25-26

Week Fifteen Reflection:

Journal your thoughts throughout the week as you reflect on the
devotional or scripture passage on the following page:

_____

_____

_____

_____

_____

_____

_____

_____

_____

_____

_____

_____

Seek His Refuge

"Trust in Him at all times, O people;
Pour out your heart before Him;
God is a refuge for us."
Psalm 62:8

Week Sixteen Reflection:

Journal your thoughts throughout the week as you reflect on the
devotional or scripture passage on the following page:

_____

_____

_____

_____

_____

_____

_____

_____

_____

_____

_____

_____

_____

My Rock and Fortress

"The Lord is my rock and my fortress
and my deliverer;
My God, my strength, in whom I will trust;
My shield and the horn of my salvation,
my stronghold."
Psalm 18:2

Week Seventeen Reflection:

Journal your thoughts throughout the week as you reflect on the devotional or scripture passage on the following page:

_____

_____

_____

_____

_____

_____

_____

_____

_____

_____

_____

Take My Tears

"You number my wanderings;
Put my tears into Your bottle;
Are they not in Your book?"
Psalm 56:8

Week Eighteen Reflection:

Journal your thoughts throughout the week as you reflect on the
devotional or scripture passage on the following page:

_____

_____

_____

_____

_____

_____

_____

_____

_____

_____

Believe in Me

"Let not your heart
be troubled;
you believe in God,
believe also in Me."

John 14:1

Week Nineteen Reflection:

Journal your thoughts throughout the week as you reflect on the
devotional or scripture passage on the following page:

_____

_____

_____

_____

_____

_____

_____

_____

_____

_____

_____

He Cares

"Therefore humble yourselves under the
mighty hand of God,
that He may exalt you in due time, casting
all your care upon Him,
for He cares for you."
1 Peter 5:6-7

Week Twenty Reflection:

Journal your thoughts throughout the week as you reflect on the devotional or scripture passage on the following page:

_____

_____

_____

_____

_____

_____

_____

_____

_____

_____

_____

A Time for Everything

"To everything there is a season, a time
for every purpose under heaven…
A time to weep, and a time to laugh;
A time to mourn,
and a time to dance."
Ecclesiastes 3:1,4

Week Twenty-One Reflection:

Journal your thoughts throughout the week as you reflect on the
devotional or scripture passage on the following page:

_____

_____

_____

_____

_____

_____

_____

_____

_____

_____

_____

_____

Prayer of Thanks

"Heavenly Father, thank You for walking with me through this journey of grief. As I face this season of sorrow, help me find comfort in remembering my loved one. Thank You for the time we had together and for the blessing of our relationship. I know You are my source for strength. Please cover me with Your peace that surpasses all understanding. Amen."

Ali Paskun

Week Twenty-Two Reflection:

Journal your thoughts throughout the week as you reflect on the devotional or scripture passage on the following page:

_____

_____

_____

_____

_____

_____

_____

_____

_____

_____

_____

_____

The Brokenhearted

"He heals the brokenhearted and binds
up their sorrows."
Psalm 147:3

Week Twenty-Three Reflection:

Journal your thoughts throughout the week as you reflect on the
devotional or scripture passage on the following page:

_____

_____

_____

_____

_____

_____

_____

_____

_____

_____

_____

A Future of Freedom

"And God will wipe away every tear from
their eyes; there shall be
no more death, nor sorrow, nor crying.
There shall be no more pain,
for the former things have passed away."
Revelation 21:4

Week Twenty-Four Reflection:

Journal your thoughts throughout the week as you reflect on the
devotional or scripture passage on the following page:

_____

_____

_____

_____

_____

_____

_____

_____

_____

_____

_____

_____

You Will Rejoice

"Therefore you now have sorrow; but I
will see you again
and your heart will rejoice, and your joy
no one will take from you."
John 16:22

Week Twenty-Five Reflection:

Journal your thoughts throughout the week as you reflect on the
devotional or scripture passage on the following page:

_____

_____

_____

_____

_____

_____

_____

_____

_____

_____

_____

_____

Joy Will Come

"For His anger is but for a moment,
His favor is for life;
Weeping may endure for a night,
But joy comes in the morning."
Psalm 30:5

Week Twenty-Six Reflection:

Journal your thoughts throughout the week as you reflect on the
devotional or scripture passage on the following page:

_____

_____

_____

_____

_____

_____

_____

_____

_____

_____

_____

_____

Death No More

"He will swallow up death forever, And
the Lord God will wipe away tears
from all faces;
The rebuke of His people
He will take away from all the earth;
For the Lord has spoken."
Isaiah 25:8

Week Twenty-Seven Reflection:

Journal your thoughts throughout the week as you reflect on the devotional or scripture passage on the following page:

_____

_____

_____

_____

_____

_____

_____

_____

_____

_____

_____

_____

Jesus, Our Friend

"If there is something we need more than
anything else during grief,
it is a friend who stands with us,
who doesn't leave us.
Jesus is that friend."

Billy Graham[3]

(American Evangelist)

Week Twenty-Eight Reflection:

Journal your thoughts throughout the week as you reflect on the devotional or scripture passage on the following page:

_____

_____

_____

_____

_____

_____

_____

_____

_____

_____

_____

_____

His Peace

"Peace I leave with you,
My peace I give to you;
not as the world gives do I give to you.
Let not your heart be troubled,
neither let it be afraid."

John 14:27

Week Twenty-Nine Reflection:

Journal your thoughts throughout the week as you reflect on the devotional or scripture passage on the following page:

_____

_____

_____

_____

_____

_____

_____

_____

_____

_____

_____

_____

He Will Save

"The Lord also will be a refuge
for the oppressed,
A refuge in times of trouble."
Psalm 9:9

Week Thirty Reflection:

Journal your thoughts throughout the week as you reflect on the devotional or scripture passage on the following page:

_____

_____

_____

_____

_____

_____

_____

_____

_____

_____

_____

_____

Do Not Be Anxious

"Be anxious for nothing, but in
everything by prayer and supplication,
with thanksgiving, let your requests be
made known to God;
and the peace of God, which surpasses all
understanding, will guard
your hearts and minds through
Christ Jesus."
Phillipians 6:7

Week Thirty-One Reflection:

Journal your thoughts throughout the week as you reflect on the devotional or scripture passage on the following page:

_____

_____

_____

_____

_____

_____

_____

_____

_____

_____

_____

_____

Find Peace

"These things I have spoken to you, that
in Me you may have peace.
In the world you will have tribulation; but
be of good cheer,
I have overcome the world."
John 16:33

Week Thirty-Two Reflection:

Journal your thoughts throughout the week as you reflect on the devotional or scripture passage on the following page:

_____

_____

_____

_____

_____

_____

_____

_____

_____

_____

_____

_____

In Spite of Grief

"We rejoice in spite of our grief, not in place of it."
Woodrow Kroll
(Evangelical Preacher)

Week Thirty-Three Reflection:

Journal your thoughts throughout the week as you reflect on the
devotional or scripture passage on the following page:

_____

_____

_____

_____

_____

_____

_____

_____

_____

_____

_____

Sow and Reap

"Those who sow in tears shall
reap in joy."
Psalm 126:5

Week Thirty-Four Reflection:

Journal your thoughts throughout the week as you reflect on the
devotional or scripture passage on the following page:

_____

_____

_____

_____

_____

_____

_____

_____

_____

_____

_____

He Trusts You

"You will keep him in perfect peace,
Whose mind is stayed on You,
Because he trusts in You."
Isaiah 26:3

Week Thirty-Five Reflection:

Journal your thoughts throughout the week as you reflect on the
devotional or scripture passage on the following page:

_____

_____

_____

_____

_____

_____

_____

_____

_____

_____

_____

Help in Trouble

"God is our refuge and strength,
A very present help in trouble."
Psalm 46:1

Week Thirty-Six Reflection:

Journal your thoughts throughout the week as you reflect on the devotional or scripture passage on the following page:

_____

_____

_____

_____

_____

_____

_____

_____

_____

_____

_____

_____

Hope in the Holy Spirit

"Now may the God of hope fill you
with all joy and peace in believing,
that you may abound in hope by the
power of the Holy Spirit."
Romans 15:13

Week Thirty-Seven Reflection:

Journal your thoughts throughout the week as you reflect on the
devotional or scripture passage on the following page:

_____

_____

_____

_____

_____

_____

_____

_____

_____

_____

_____

_____

Prayer of Praise

"You are the Lord who gives comfort to the grieving, hope to the hopeless, and shelter to the lost.
I bring my sorrow to you now to receive Your comfort, hope, and shelter. I praise You for Your faithfulness to all who believe and Your promise to never forsake us, especially during the times we are walking through the valley.
In Jesus most Precious and Holy name. Amen."

Ali Paskun

Week Thirty-Eight Reflection:

Journal your thoughts throughout the week as you reflect on the devotional or scripture passage on the following page:

_____

_____

_____

_____

_____

_____

_____

_____

_____

_____

_____

_____

_____

_____

_____

_____

Listen, He's Calling

"Pain insists upon being attended to. God
whispers to us in our pleasures, speaks in
our consciences, but shouts in our pains.
It is his megaphone to rouse
a deaf world."

C. S. Lewis[5]

(British writer, lay theologian, and scholar)

Week Thirty-Nine Reflection:

Journal your thoughts throughout the week as you reflect on the
devotional or scripture passage on the following page:

_____

_____

_____

_____

_____

_____

_____

_____

_____

_____

_____

Power and Love

"When we view today through the grid of eternity,
the sting of grief is dulled by His power and love.
Consistently meditating on God's redemption and
our secure future in heaven has the power to set us
free when grief is holding us back."
David Jeremiah[6]
(Senior pastor of Shadow Mountain
Community Church)

Week Forty Reflection:

Journal your thoughts throughout the week as you reflect on the
devotional or scripture passage on the following page:

_____

_____

_____

_____

_____

_____

_____

_____

_____

_____

_____

Don't Suffer

"Suffering is unbearable if you aren't
certain that God is for you and with you."

Timothy Keller[7]

(Author of *Walking with God through Pain and
Suffering*)

Week Forty-One Reflection:

Journal your thoughts throughout the week as you reflect on the devotional or scripture passage on the following page:

_____

_____

_____

_____

_____

_____

_____

_____

_____

_____

_____

Help in Our Weakness

"He will swallow up death forever, And the Lord
God will wipe away tears from all faces;
The rebuke of His people
He will take away from all the earth;
For the Lord has spoken."
Romans 8:26

Week Forty-Two Reflection:

Journal your thoughts throughout the week as you reflect on the devotional or scripture passage on the following page:

_____

_____

_____

_____

_____

_____

_____

_____

_____

_____

_____

_____

Snuggle with God

"Snuggle in God's arms. When you are hurting, when you feel lonely, left out.
Let Him cradle you, comfort you, reassure you of His all-sufficient power and love."

Kay Arthur[8]

(American Christian Bible teacher, co-founder of Precept Ministries International, Author)

Week Forty-Three Reflection:

Journal your thoughts throughout the week as you reflect on the devotional or scripture passage on the following page:

You're Not Alone

"You don't have to be alone in your hurt! Comfort is
yours. Joy is an option. And it's all been made
possible by your Savior. He went without comfort so
you might have it. He postponed joy so you might
share in it. He willingly chose isolation so you might
never be alone in your hurt and sorrow."

Joni Eareckson Tada[9]
(American evangelical Christian author, artist, and
founder of Joni and Friends)

Week Forty-Four Reflection:

Journal your thoughts throughout the week as you reflect on the devotional or scripture passage on the following page:

_____

_____

_____

_____

_____

_____

_____

_____

_____

_____

_____

_____

He Shows Compassion

"Though he brings grief, he will show
compassion,
so great is his unfailing love."
Lamentations 3:32-33

Week Forty-Five Reflection:

Journal your thoughts throughout the week as you reflect on the devotional or scripture passage on the following page:

_____

_____

_____

_____

_____

_____

_____

_____

_____

_____

_____

_____

The Lord Goes First

"The Lord himself goes before you and
will be with you; he will never leave you
nor forsake you.
Do not be afraid;
do not be discouraged."
Deuteronomy 31:8

Week Forty-Six Reflection:

Journal your thoughts throughout the week as you reflect on the devotional or scripture passage on the following page:

_____

_____

_____

_____

_____

_____

_____

_____

_____

_____

_____

_____

_____

In Our Midst

"The Lord your God is in your midst, a
mighty one who will save;
He will rejoice over you with gladness;
He will quiet you by his love;
he will exult over you with loud singing."
Zephaniah 3:17

Week Forty-Seven Reflection:

Journal your thoughts throughout the week as you reflect on the devotional or scripture passage on the following page:

_____

_____

_____

_____

_____

_____

_____

_____

_____

_____

_____

_____

God Is Mighty

"In the midst of grief, it is critical for us to remember that the God who is sovereign and mighty is also Immanuel – God with us."

Pastor Jon Nelson[10]

(Author of *Moving Forward: Walking though Grief*)

Week Forty-Eight Reflection:

Journal your thoughts throughout the week as you reflect on the devotional or scripture passage on the following page:

_____

_____

_____

_____

_____

_____

_____

_____

_____

_____

_____

Walking with Us

"When our grief is debilitating and it feels impossible to function, God does not sit aloof in heaven. He does not leave us to figure out how to handle grief on our own or how to cast about for resources to get through it. He walks every step of the journey with us."

Elizabeth Groves[11]
(Author of the Article "Grief and the Christian")

Week Forty-Nine Reflection:

Journal your thoughts throughout the week as you reflect on the
devotional or scripture passage on the following page:

_____

_____

_____

_____

_____

_____

_____

_____

_____

_____

_____

He Will Be with You

"When you pass through the waters,
I will be with you;
and when you pass through the rivers,
they will not sweep over you.
When you walk through the fire, you will
not be burned;
the flames will not set you ablaze."

Isaiah 43:2

Week Fifty Reflection:

Journal your thoughts throughout the week as you reflect on the devotional or scripture passage on the following page:

_____

_____

_____

_____

_____

_____

_____

_____

_____

_____

His Love Endures

"For I am convinced that neither death
nor life, neither angels nor demons,
neither the present nor the future, nor any
powers, neither height nor depth, nor
anything else in all creation, will be able to
separate us from the love of God that is
in Christ Jesus our Lord."
Romans 8:38-39

Week Fifty-One Reflection:

Journal your thoughts throughout the week as you reflect on the devotional or scripture passage on the following page:

_____

_____

_____

_____

_____

_____

_____

_____

_____

_____

_____

_____

Prayer of Hope

"Holy Spirit, guide me through this valley of grief.
Remind me of the hope I have in Christ,
the hope of eternal life and reunion with my
loved ones. Thank You, Lord, for Your everlasting
love and for the promise of Your peace that
surpasses all understanding. May Your grace sustain
me, and Your light guide me through the darkness.
In Jesus' name, Amen."

Ali Paskun

Week Fifty-Two Reflection:

Journal your thoughts throughout the week as you reflect on the devotional or scripture passage on the following page:

_____

_____

_____

_____

_____

_____

_____

_____

_____

_____

_____

_____

In Closing...

"Lord, We lift up those who are grieving, asking for Your comfort and peace to surround them. In their sorrow, may they feel Your loving presence. Strengthen them, Lord, as they navigate this difficult time. Grant them the hope of eternal life and the assurance that their loved ones are in Your care. May Your grace sustain them, and may they find solace in Your unfailing love.
In Jesus' name. Amen."

Ali Paskun

More Journaling Space

If you need more space to write about your feelings when it comes to your grief, the following pages offer a place where you can journal your thoughts and feelings.

_____

_____

_____

_____

_____

_____

_____

_____

_____

_____

_____

_____

_____

_____

_____

References

1. Guthrie, N. (2017, May 29) *Six Words to Say Through Tears: The Source of Comfort in the Pain of Grief.* desiringGod.org. https://www.desiringgod.org/articles/six-words-to-say-through-tears

2. Graham, B. (2004, July 9) *The Healer of Our Broken Hearts.* billygraham.org. https://billygraham.org/story/the-healer-of-our-broken-hearts/

3. Kroll, W. https://bibleportal.com/bible-quote/grief-joy-we-rejoice-in-spite-of-our-grief-not-in-place-of-it

4. Ritchie, D. (2017, January 16) God Shouts to Us in Our Pain. desiringGod.org. https://www.desiringgod.org/articles/god-shouts-to-us-in-our-pain/

5. Jeremiah, D. The Loss of a Loved One: Moving from Grief to Hope. davidjeremiah.blog. https://davidjeremiah.blog/the-loss-of-a-loved-one-moving-from-grief-to-hope/

6. Keller, T, 2013, *Walking with God through Pain and Suffering,* Penguin Books.

7. Arthury, K, 1995, *My Savior, My Friend: A Daily Devotional,* Harvest House Publishers.

8. Joni Eareckson Tada, Joni and Friends, https://www.christianquotes.info/quotes-by-author/joni-eareckson-tada-quotes/

9. Nelson, J. Moving Forward: Walking though Grief. somajc.org. https://somajc.org/walking-though-grief/

10. Groves, E. (2015, December 25) Grief and the Christian. ligonier.org. https://www.ligonier.org/learn/articles/grief-and-christian

About the Author

Ali Paskun accepted the Lord's gift of salvation
in 2006. She began living with grief when her
husband Bill went home in 2014 after twenty-
seven years of marriage. Relying on faith in
Jesus Christ helped her; she now wishes to help
others realize the strength and peace that comes
from resting in the arms of a loving Savior.
As a member of the 420 Fire Maryland Church,
Ali teaches regularly to train and equip
other disciples.